Storm Crop

Stacie Leatherman

Storm Crop

Stacie Leatherman

BlazeVOX [books]

Buffalo, New York

Published by BlazeVOX [books]

Printed in the United States of America

Book design by Geoffrey Gatza

Cover image: *Rowan leaves laid around hole/collecting the last few leaves/nearly finished/dog ran
into hole/ started again/made in the shade on a windy, sunny day* © Andy Goldsworthy
Courtesy Galerie Lelong, New York

First Edition
ISBN: 978-1-60964-051-4
Library of Congress Control Number 2010939081

BlazeVOX [books]
303 Bedford Ave
Buffalo, NY 14216

Editor@blazevox.org

publisher of weird little books

BlazeVOX [books]

blazevox.org

2   4   6   8   0   9   7   5   3   1

BlazeVOX

Acknowledgments

My gratitude to the editors of the following publications, in which these poems first appeared:

BlazeVOX: "B," "C," and "E"

Caketrain: "D" and "R"

Cricket Online Review: "J"

Diagram: "A"

elimae: "M," "N," "P," and "Q"

Interim: "Y"

isotope: "G"

Lamination Colony: "F" and "L"

New American Writing: "H"

Packingtown Review: "X"

Spinning Jenny: "I"

SUB-LIT: "S," "T," "U" and "W"

Thank you as well to Geoffrey Gatza, not only for supporting this book, but for supporting the literary community. To my husband Michael Hemery, thank you for giving me the space and time to write, and for trusting my work, and I thank you for never again allowing a bazooka-toting chipmunk to enter its pages. And thank you to my loved ones, especially Kathy Hemery for giving me the Most Publishable Poet Award all those years ago, and to Dan Hemery, because of your clear and unflinching parental love, and whose purity of mind and heart is, indeed, a salvation.

Contents

To us

" ...if
in time we see
the words fail this
we know this
we walk in and is all
we know we
will speak

to each
other we
will speak"

—George Oppen, from "Neighbors"

"The infants and the animals
And the insects
'stare at the open'

And she said
Therefore they are welcome."

—George Oppen, from "Quotations"

Storm Crop

A

A

the body's metric, a is home not home,

not the end but the anarchic, semantic crust,

re-toweling of thought, filament,

lots of how you say, conservation,

A the ancient way of paying bills,

you know, dying. A for birds of paradise,

ribbon-tailed. A is I refuse to say

the source. Any not-yet-tied aspects.

This the book not the book.

What I hold up merely a part,

bird flies in threads out

feather through a tribesman's nose.

Wave pool. Landing pad,

departure point, and the tarmacs inbetween.

Hand over hand the clothesline drawn in,

alight here and take something away,

alight here and bring something back.

If violence is necessary

we will discuss in small voices,

skeptical hands.

In the dead corners

dancing bear, snout threaded with rope.

Jerked up from the dusty road

by the alphabet's nose,

letters resound   snarl and curse,

Deep exhaustion of serving.

A is for order. Paradox.

A for the before that was never before.

Belief.

To be lost in meaning, all entry points,

the supernatural speaking in your ear,

with it, A the great woe,

What animals do not fit the bill?

extended   shrunk,

my gored nose fills with pollen,

Time the texture, silent trumpet song.

de-syntaxed. What language crux?

Necessity of beginning.

The healed wound.

Unmapped directions.

Any alphabet one wishes to choose.

A the exit, A the raunchy song,

A the logic of longing, I speak with this,

the scattering.

Time can be crossed and knotted

bouquets of it I sniff and sniff,

bees buzz about my brows.

I hear it in the call. What passes

              like an orchard—

B

B

Dear B,

No straight way, I'm afraid.
Letters from the dead to the living.

Washing. Warbling. Where are we going but sidestream.
Secondary, stationary, no, the hierarchy's moot.
Dear B, don't get me started. The repetition.

The constellation of it.

The shift. When there's something that needs be said
but too many ways to say it. The line out your own.
The fragments.
The letters standing at your side.

Dear B, we go past. Rangings true as migration.
The traveling companion. Dear B, our arraignment.
The hearkening. The hymn. The Braille of it. Hummingbird wings.
The instantaneous.

It's all in the address. How privileged to cast a shadow,
to be the shadow. How we filibuster night's edge.
But night has no edge, B. Night's all ridges. Dunes.
Confrontation in my blood, but bear me close. It's iffy.
What drives an animal to murder. Any, it seems, has the potential.
We are not original. The bearing out.
The bearing. The daily bric a brac, borders and boycotts...

Dear B, the ambuscade, road slick like mucous. Luminosity.

Unfinished business. Childhood tightens its belt.
Childhood tired of the human. I want to cross, want to let cross.
We need a rogue arrangement. The assonance goes without saying.

Dear B, the bursting door. Quiet step within. Earthquake, boot,
peninsula sinking, ankles wet, bodies floating away.

You have the ring of the penultimate. A circular motion, an orbit.
You the myth and truth. The precious. B the love I feel
in capital letters. The sheer output.

B, the downpour. Move. Blinking the eye will shed sand out sometimes.
The thing is, we're inextricable. At all points one picks up,
at all points one is lost. The lost find the lost.
The distance in the grass from me to you.
B the incessance. I wish for the unabridged edition.
In case of emergency we will taxi in.

C

C

Living has a dynamite effect. Chants depart and migrate, live in the folds, the instigation moving. We saw each other and gasped. Transformation, that C. It's all been done before. Who wants the bravado? Much to say about our times, the specifics, the rigamarole. Though clusters I like. Real, complete sentences. Anarchic scents, though routine a godsend. If you're there in the recount, run. Hellbent I understand. Linguistic contraptions, the air we breathe potent as seed. I said the dead change as much as the living, that living isn't the only way of telling the truth. Heat blows through the house like a stranger. That sound a spider in your ear.

Rankling. Some people lock themselves down tight, nuclear shelters, secure from everyone but themselves. Being tardy is relevant. There are no longer such things as roads. There are invisibilities. Refusals. Scant ghosts.

I want to live in the exteriority. The reconnaissance mission. What about its compactness is not genius? What if I'm inflicting again? Sweeping. I would like someone to sweep strong but gently and with open door and the broom itself to open so not a broom at all but a steady wind. Oops a daisy. The real estate complete. What phobia do you have? C for all body parts, body poets I accidentally wrote. Cry out loud, cryptic, there's a separateness, a balloon ride high above, a gas explosion, a rising away from but a need to keep tethered to; will C seem changed because I've changed? Will it execute in the same way? Will I ask it the same questions? Will I rely upon it? Will I ask it to regard its subject differently, always?

Who told you about last night? Whose hand can you shake when most everyone is dealt a bad hand? Who is it that defends you when you can't trust the hand you're given?

D

D

Rhapsody. Mispronunciations. What is it about childhood that affects us. A plane homing in.
The denunciation, the informant. Keep it close. The razzle dazzle. The dark authorial voice.
Nose up. Arrow. Demolition, defrocked, demilitarized, Frankensteined. Lever up the shiny
stuff past 10 o'clock. Entrance grants sanctity. *Duende*, demarcation. And the living doesn't
portrait as well as you might think. D so close to the cusp. The confusion, the paradox.
Devotion. The evidence against us. We fly our own way, though living has its possibilities.
Desolitude. Desegregation of souls. Poor Pythagoras, except for your theorem, mostly lost.
The antipathy, the feint. Appropriation of grief something natural here. I'm drawn to it like
wings to light. Sharp percolations. Positive identification. Lifted windows like lifted skirts, the
lock, stock, and barrel. The blessings are mixed. In bloom, call girls are asking you for paper to
write it all down. We are forever writing with our bodies. I *can* make sense of it. Danger a
mother lode. The grandiloquent, the dry eye, the seemings ripped, the fusion confused, the
cheerful bruise, antagonism, desire...

Eventually D knocks, we want nothing to do with it. The living are stuck with the living, dead
to the dead. Now face the other. The evil wicks away (hardly at all). Bad fabric? D in the
darkness D in the light. For words that begin with D in other languages. Where maybe D
doesn't exist at all. Proto chango. Sediment, siding. The unilateral nature of anything, which is
complete, utter denial. Immeasurability that can be measured. Infinitely. Underestimation,
priceless. The embitterment, pure power. Prolixity on time. Lift off happened hours ago,
minutes ago, now, futurity. The future full of maturity. Imminence. An image dismantled.
Immense forgetfulness. We not that important and of the utmost, still proving our DNA.
Prowling around. The idea to hold off. To aggress. Pursue. We've been underpinned, lifebloods
of silence. We do not always choose the things we need to do. Alluvial, bright...

Yet bury me in time for dinner. Traditional measurements of time that I so desperately need.
Don't get me wrong, I exist within the parameters. There are two ways at least this can go.
You fill in the rest; it's a constant revision. The decisions we make, if we're lucky, are our own.
It's an interesting conceit. The versus, the verisimilitude are remarkable. Enough is enough.
No resurrection except in hushes, disbelief. Welcome to our planet. Please buckle in. The
iridescent flicker of wings. What season. Monarchs clinging. Our dues. No fleeing the outpost
before too late.

I need the ghost word. Leaf prints in cement. Something there, weaving. And the bruisings. The under sea level. Levees, pumps, dams. Who will we find above the gravestone, waiting. To survive is the only prerequisite, the final exam. I cannot complain. Not a matter of when, but how. How dapper. Delinquent. A small intimate concert at 8 p.m. Boisterous hummings coming clear. Compass points, libations, love sketched in pencil; it's emphatic! Clusters of photographs like strophes, bundlings of nerves, package deal. Is it erratic to write in one long perfect line so we feel all evening gown? Desire in fields, folds. The field notes say: each section of this is domestic, a magnet. A freezer full of good oaths, a bedtime story. Did you tell it? Did it find its lucky day?

E

E

Clipping of the spine. Random assassinations. Run away with someone like, but not, me. Who will defile you when I'm no longer here? Will you consider this a death threat? Who will follow, place you under house arrest? Who will stay to be realized? Who is not fascinating in their humdrum tyranny? Who deserves to have her ponytail tied in knots? Who will expatiate? Who can't suffer enough? Who can't arm themselves against the armistice of love? Who will not run away screaming? Who will remove her own throat? Who will offer nothing to the gods? Who is afraid to say so? Who does not fit any descriptions? Isn't it harvest? Isn't it colloquial? What do we need to survive in a way that's survivable? Will it happen like something shorn?

*

The worms of desire. Hard wired for hope. Where does one draw the moral line? Are we meant to abandon? Did I want something, they say, to speak of? Did I lift it up like a relic, a halo? Was I guilty of inconstancy? Was I the sought after, the grief? The sticking point? The washed up, the cretin, the erogenous zone? Was I the stone that delivered the stones to my body? Was I the question? Was I forgotten, was part of me swept up? Was I fossil or thread? Was I the rangy one, the fleet-footed? Was I the one who stumbled? Was I a bet cashed in? The spell that cast you under? Was I sure of my place? Was I irresolvable? Destabilized? Was I the wrong number? The shadow? The honest woman? Was I the iron maiden, the dark letterpress? Was I the germane snippet? The extolled? Was I the bolt of winter lightning, the story, the animal? Did I do it for the long haul? Did I try to find my way? Was I the golden one? The leaf falling? Did we find the right calibration? Did we send the sign? Was I the sudden implement? The carrier? Was I the bones crackling? The pull of strings? Was I the one that remained? Will I look at you again with just that configuration?

*

The voltage of waking. Did I trip the wires? Did no one learn the language again? Was I a willing accomplice? Was I the opposites attract? The operatic moment? Am I the governor of my loneliness? Am I the arch villain? Should I never have brought you here? Should we call the cops? How have the rest adapted? Is what doing fine? Will someone need us? At what point in time is there no crisis? How good am I at hollering? What is the size of one's voice? Who needs to be addressed? Who finds the shell-shocked? Who croons? Who performs the erasure? Who is atonal? Apocryphal? Loose canonical? Hymnotic?

F

F

Interwading. The virility. The tucking in sometimes.
Happy trash. Overlapping labels, projects, wires.
Disorderly like rumpled morning hair. Somehow
I have exceeded the page with longings.

The roundnesses unite. A colossus. Fret and fury. Find and comfort me.
Remember the frontal, orthodontal truth. Skinny fictions. The milk moustache of rage.
I shift to include you in the pinch and clutch. The dignity of loss, of absolution.
I shake like a front line.

What if the recondite mission is more difficult because understood.
What if I understood it all and would choose to undo it.
What if wonder meant that much.
And if the songs are true? What if stars tell you everything you need to know?

They can be aroused as I am aroused.
Kernels of light
of needing to find the right groundswell.
The effect of life upon life.

It seems the opening keeps on opening,
if you choose not to remember, it forces itself upon you in some way,
clam cracked on an otter's belly, this is the way love gets in.
Remember that seamlessness.

I would like to learn your definition of frontier.
I know infatuation. The lightning bolt that rang up everything like a
glowing bowl the other night. The United Conversation.
Everywhere people are talking. Four-leaf clovers, lucky hearts.

And truly red, each day awakens. What provocations make you salivate?
If I remember something infinite, tell me. If I can retain the memory
of the dead without recalling them. Thought and precinct.
Of use is something more pliable, an erotic position.

Enough of the introductions.
What's the speech of sand?

G

G

Friction.

How does one articulate except by attempt?

Blood loud as language.

The fuselage intact. The rain hasn't damaged us. We report for duty. We heed the call.

Grief translucent, grief like rain, forecast.

To be held in orbit, to be held.

The story always revises itself.

Electric lines, paw prints. Fading.

Sun pours light over the tall wheat-colored grasses.

Grief having no straight shot? The usual rubrics?

This bit of shale.

I am a communication. A profound suckling.

The heathen season, the he/she of it, the it of it.

Theloopings...

Precision, my dear,

isn't everything.

H

H

Bombs of love, international exchange.

I the eyelid of the universe, the back yard, what I long to capsize.

The lark, the bruise. The unfolding the empty folds and the receiving.

The triumphant horizon. The scattering of dust and color. I the reception,

the interrupt. The polyphonic, the cat sleuthing past.

No torment put to rest. Colors arrayed in their finest distinctions.

*

If we could just come close to the resuscitation.

Ghosts that travel along electric wires, whisper.

Leftovers thrown to the bones,

the dead whisper over everything they touch,

cartons and clothing,

they come as water, leaves blown across the yard,

in the gesture of lifting glass to mouth.

Shouldn't we have some excerpt that would enlighten us.

You must help yourself to seconds or starve,

be the villain, stab your neighbor's heart and survive.

You have to learn the other way, everything

they tell you, everything you abhor. This the sight

of trailing footprints and mud and snow. Birds sang underground,

cardinal passed into cloud. All around no one thought of reprimand.

I walked away guiltless with no evidence in hand.

Here the umbilical power lines at work,

here and there pines give off a green glow.

I swim around in my veins like a well-tended fish.

*

Witness as blossom.

As first pressure of rain, wind to lift and scatter,

petals borne across the yard like details from a story

that cannot be forgotten.

No one conscripted except everything,

gathering intelligence.

The abstract lives in places I can touch,

the wrist you curl round my hip each morning.

I the stand of zinnias blooming in summer fields.

You remember if I touched you there, or there.

You remember yourself scratched into trees, cement.

In working order we depart, leaving scent behind but making

lighter footprints, untracking ourselves among thistle and shrub, until we become invisible, or interesting, or both.

*

Out where band-aids, flotillas exist on the polarizations?

And where would we find the patrol car sweeping the vision of our night?

Fear a night bird, a day bird, a genius paper cut. My belly big as the anonymous.

These not dreams but the spaces within dreams, and between.

We're all done in like a detail.

The abandonment fierce and so is the condemnation.

No more will I sweep up the glass.

I suspect some espionage,

something specific you will want to relate to your next of kin,

the bid for your pebbled heart skipped across water.

Eventually you will bear backwards to the future. I am listening,

penetrating as only the deepest comedies can.

I

I

When I write of the freest subjects you can assume that I mean you.

We're so far away in our elopement

I should not even mention the connection.

Assume your ear delicate as cherry blossom,

assume the worst translations.

Expect me always to arouse the leaves of longing.

Blossoms blowing where they blow, traffic speeding out of sight.

The dead, coming back as leaves,

bearing all the green they can carry.

This the love I bear you, to come laden,

as if to cover the world.

Love is in the specifics, beer held in the

young man's hand as he mows his lawn.

In the surplus split open bags,

the returning ship that never really left at all.

There is room for love amongst this extra skin.

Pack it within the belly, in thighs your lover breathes into,

all your favorite places to be touched. And we touch you,

we smell the body aching and fragrant, as the once again and always, love packed into ourselves and drifting out,

carried not away but to and from.

*

Wing-thrum in my belly.

The potential has a knee up.

The geography of childhood indelible.

Relentless giantisms.

Reconnect tusk to tusk stump,

bodies defect from death. And they roam over us again.

Blooms in late winter, crocus head suffragettes.

We can go the long way yonder.

*

By gesture I mean genital.

By entrance I mean reciprocity.

No division between the woods meandering and your mind.

The body's stitchings do not lie.

Which are the unfolding.

I know you love me because I'm in the interim, in the closet of openness,

I'm open armed.

I the inviolate non-borders, the aid let in.

What roots of measurement shall we have in this new world?

In this domain are all domains.

In this sense of proprietorship are the remains. In these opened walls

are the dementia, the resuscitation, the milling and suspect ones,

oblique and torrential.

*

You do understand the indignation. The iconography.

Who has the power to translate? To undermine or exfoliate crimes?

I have the power to be broken.

All it takes is a squeeze of the hand.

Not many opportunities except in death,

the conjugal visits so close to home.

Scent of locust in front and behind,

maple helicopters whirring down rotor spinning,

I the same being over and over, accumulating speed and velocity

though slower today, rounder pregnant and with less momentum.

I walk a straight line and am dissatisfied.

I trip over a rock and understand where I live,

slough through dead leaves and understand ankle deep.

The method of communication:

if the derailing if the disrobing

if the violence has done us apart

if the hemorrhage won't clear

if the grass is blown backwards into its recent past,

if love is to flower as wind

if I transcend the hollowing.

Rhythm that dilates, that requests.

Deer thismorning wanderingthrough, all the ways of telling stories undone.

Gentling the erasure,

I have my establishments,

the indivisible,

the interruption, the breath you just exhaled.

J

J

And then we chatter fierce,

live wires flipping

lip's shelter,

throat's cave,

I'm not long for another world.

No understanding except seeds,

rind, carvings,

scent and retrievals

the underachievement of the senses

that calls daily for you to bloom,

heal the unwieldy wound that quivers, falls out of itself,

requires tucking back into, pink and obstinate, accidental.

The breeze kicking under thin leaves.

Sometimes I hear clear across train tracks,

now few

the secret

grassy expanses

This.

I have left off where I began.

Backwards as I am forwards

shining,

you see me everywhere all at once scientific and sensuous.

Dive,

foot caught in rope, I'm saved

by accident.

The last time, this time, overhead, aurora.

Consolidated by another being.

Allium, globular, indeed we are circular I bend

back and touch my toes.

Let us be the offertory, the humm-nal, the tune rearranged.

The waiting,

the oblique happiness,

self at seed's end blown out

and leaving the shell

as if washed on a beach

no less

beautiful than ten lionesses on the flanks and sides of an elephant,

letters and teeth aflame.

I joyous.

Someone picks up after, a relay, the hand off.

The body escapes and escapes depending on context.

Each day one foot in front of the other, which is politics, rebellion.

The quiet accumulations. Of rain, small disasters,

cawings of air, gauzy sky.

Subtleties, misfit interpretations,

perhaps the simplest language is best.

The traffic of grass.

To be precise is to survive, but sometimes the utterance saves you.

A circle opens in all directions.

We move so far away from the internal gestures.

And we become and then we turn,

climb from the land of the living

to the land of the living.

Each being its own narrative.

The sky listing forth. I cringe at the impeccability.

I understand something of danger, the slow knock at the front door,

the usual plagiarisms.

But what is spoken isn't meant to keep.

The fragrance you wear on your wrist is me.

The child wakes like the alphabet,

gestures, scrawls himself into the landscape.

I feel his belief in darkness and sound,

in what happens beneath.

There is no other here.

K

K

We're revised as we speak.

To attune.

Kitsch, of course. Kites and high-flying plutocracies.

The body's lace its organs the child beating within.

It lifts like a sunburn and I am borne into it.

The finesse of loving, as if relationships could be held in tow.

The long sidewalks to hell and back,

straight and smooth as a syringe.

And where someone or the self pulls us off,

a light wave, a frequency.

The process of something we once knew.

Your lowing cattling us through the night.

You find the trails strong as any writing.

Iron horsed,

the bad luck fruition,

the clustering, the badlands,

ribbon fish, you glide through like a transition,

your body sliced more than half your length,

a cut thread, swimming.

*

The dead over under us, at eye level.

I refuse to discuss in separations. I am not my own language utterly.

Doors and wounds, disappearances, returns.

Reliance on hands, mind, teeth.

*

The drifting backwards into disrepair,

the unclotting, the swift dislocation.

The swifter we go.

Drift of continents and islands.

Words threshed, chaff from grain.

Updraft, uprising.

Words catching in the backdraft.

*

If a collision, or elision, or what has clapped silently above me.

The knots tying it together.

Spring flowers dusting ditches and roads,

you walk,

cottonwood blowing like the sifted alphabet,

the approach of solstice.

Light as the waiting and receiving.

The kissing words backwards until they have breath.

Until a flock breaking upwards in flight,

the sky breathing, insistence of motion and intent and wandering.

Seeds scattering, a spume,

an umbrella of sparks.

*

The signing of the entire body,

the circular motions.

Your body's lamplight.

The last time is not the last time.

*

There is the painful retaliation.

The crosshairs.

The splitting of,

the close shave.

*

Lightning a savage crop,

fierce as your broken heart.

Inchworm inching across my arm,

contracting

the crashing and impetuosity.

Slouch erected straight as a wave curling over,

the origami of moments,

beach gored with light.

The unknown more intimate,

under the finger in the lung.

L

L

I fit something inside your suitcase the size of a dime
which will cause you pain. Your dog yammers on and tells your secrets.
You the hate mail. The most anguished person to be desired. An anathema.

I've no ear for your brick hallelujahs. Who plans to take the glass from your lips
and walk you out before anyone can suggest otherwise?
Who will kick you from the cliff? What's the taste of shipwreck?

The sloop of guilt, that fancy dancer, moves through back rooms, a tyrant,
no need for the particulars, simply apply one's life version here,
rat a tat touille, effervescent. The moon, pale poker chip in the sky.

But who's counting, anyway? Any sort of superstition we can address here, boys?
At the intersection, do you love me? Do you know the code word?
If in any case you cannot handle the precociousness of the situation,

the caves will arch your back. All is going as well as can be expected.
The gumption. Our radiating influence. Who walks off wearing the habit.
Who swears to the end. Life simply a conversion. I am constantly awry.

And routine checkups hurt; don't let them fool you. Time a tricky word,
all negligence, negligee and beef. I am under the impression you like to have sex.
That you'd perform it with me like an execution,

a cotillion, a pasture of dusk. Make love like a glacier and raze.
How political to want to die. How stringent the playing field.
I am nothing, but that doesn't cover it. Even after the lechery,

we're compatible. Where did you lay us out?
No use getting hung up on the details—
I won't see you at the bottom though we'll both be there.

Lies like leotards cling. Do you want to circulate? Even lichen speaks,
trees communicate and defend. Who in the heavens listens
in on such intimate conversations? How is this all going to mutate?

The ecosystem of longing, the daily taxonomy? We have this imaginary address.

I haven't been too bad, have I? Over under through all the letters,
cross referencing handy after all. The rough surgery,

the unthought-of complications, the ramshackle noise of us,
ransacked, the troubled spewing, the click of bowls,
bones, their twinkling, suggestive tones,

gator eats python splits in half, how does one survive agony,
become what we call desensitized, omniscient, fly's eye,
the stained glass, the broken and whole, the mosaic of water.

Obsessions grow like the questionable parts.
The book shaken out and emptied. The book gaining speed.
The intricacies of death, its rotund possibilities.

The lies of daily living, one foot in front of the other,
the privilege of doing so, looking up at the apprehended sky.
Leavings, the grand colorations. The political is what?

Resurrection has its ominous tone. I am full of the landscape,
the specific habitats, the lab rats.
This that this that fulcrum. I am the softest taking down.

The line between us hard to draw
I keep gliding over and over,
truth between us told.

Leaves rustle over cached animals,
bioluminescence, rhubarb, flute.
Love comes back fully reported in the end

a secret that travels but remains secret
until kept by everyone.
I wouldn't have called it a mistake,

this love, this crop. Instead, a simple misspelling.
The slurring of boundaries. If we belch and rocket,
who will tend the garden and collect rainwater,

who will bend it all connect? Our bodies' drawl,
mixing of species long isolated from each other—
The sun is shining deep into the earth as I move beneath you.

In the light we disappear.
If stopped at the border we row through in our boat of wishes.
Hope which is your split hand.

Hope, a hook. A benchwarmer,
a surrogate,
the sultry condition.

Do you dream in fish? Hang upside down from claws the size of dreams?
There's so much anonymity in existence except
that you might be perceived by every single thing.

M

M

The need for story.

Anyone within range concussive,

presence of body the oracular,

the disappearing.

Waiting for the next tension.

If you're here in the recount, breathe.

If you make it through the wind tunnels,

windows jagged open...

*

The bodies are indeed embedded.

I flip towards you, a car out of control.

*

The need for new violences?

The body showing its heat like a mirage.

The horror of the small and unguarded places.

The smooth-skinned whale of fact.

The ship lists left then right.

By now the world is realigned.

You cannot go back to touch us, the dead,

you can only find us in approximations,

nothing like the heft of your hand, now, upon your cheek,

your body in its long bed of light.

*

There is nothing that can't be ground in, they say.

Morning glory of trash truck screeching by,

transfer station, incinerator or landfill,

seagulls screaming.

Hand-made missions.

I have lots of tinkering to do.

Always transitions, the leachate,

lies bloated in the streets.

The irony is hard, hand grated.

Not the making but the turning out.

Did I arrange my shoulders in an appropriate posture of delay?

The separation of life from life.

The bowing of head and tail.

We still churning on the hooks.

N

N

No wonderments left except in your extended hand?

It is enough.

A burning connect,

reconfiguration of the letter.

About the odds of resilience.

The way the home is built from remnants,

winter's maiden grass,

for hatchlings expert in hunger.

We will be reborn as particles or some other consequence.

I do believe in the assassinations of belief.

Nesting in the blizzard places.

Interludes.

Three heartbeats now, one nested into the other.

We stretch into separate sleeps.

The love of the potential,

there's no mouth against such circumstances.

You're powerless before the efficacy, such fragile flight,

words broken up over the ocean.

Move over. The entities that abrupt you cannot be reconciled.

But the nesting continues, head within head, heart within heart.

Grief like forgiveness.

The mission twist,

foot cramp making you hop in agony, your heart upon wakening,

show me what is within,

the incubation.

Nests within nests,

trap doors

each a burst of feathers and flight—

O

O

You can dislocate bone but not the memory of bone.

P

P

We could speak over a delicate meal of excuses.

Everything I can use up, against deadlines.

I swear this will be the last time I remind you.

The judicious blend and the outcomes sizzling.

The paparazzi haven't a clue.

Try to say something intimate.

Punitive damages. Penmanship. Figure out fruition.

Unrig the offerings.

The buoyancy of lies.

Of misunderstandings, how they direct traffic, signal dead zones.

The trash talk I associate with you.

Of the never say never again.

Penultimate is like that.

The mouth of the wild,

beauty the stoutness of its intent.

The trust one gives when attempting entrance and exit.

The mind misspeaking is honest.

I can hold the pose of your approval.

Touch the inconsequential,

fumigate, arrange for the well to do,

pet the skulls of suffering,

arithmetic the fall—

Q

Q

The sorrow felt beyond borders.

Attending is the detail.

Bedside manner critical.

The undermining.

Seal the details like wax

they will melt and pour into another form

no more perfect than the other.

*

The shape of reliance, the interrogation.

The opulence, the quick kiss.

The furthermost point of undressed.

The pelt of outrunning.

The arrangement grossly precarious.

There isn't a way you aren't affected.

To gather like propaganda.

My artillery of grain,

inheritance, infiltration.

Let's not fault the arrangement, the dottings.

There isn't a commendation we haven't heard before,

flesh snagged in teeth.

I serve you wishes on a stick that I dissolve upon offering.

Hope a bludgeon.

Heart a pistol gleaming,

enervated through indignation, patrols.

There, in your kiss, a greater anxiety.

You scrape out your domain;

I mean for this to be a banner year.

R

R

Not a chance in flowering hell. Tambourines bashing near your head.
The arc. I understand little, but gaze in all directions like a fly.

I want the safe distance. We the tenuous, causing. Requiem the dying language's language.
Brisk business. Billboards, each movement each utterance requiem,

every action counteraction prayers spinning overhead, contraction of bodies,
longing, willing what must be willed, for which no answer, no belief.

A wave of the hand, passing of grief, the inexplicability,
the dead past us, feral. Prayer every act of grief an animal can make,

open ended and overtaxed. Drunken telephone calls. Early wakenings.
The diameter of grief no one really knows except…

The restoration. Final resting place wherever one falls, was felled. The stripping.
Take this go swiftly, you already gone—)

what I hope can overtake you at the gate, requiem not something bound by definition, bread
not bread, but bird. Careful of even your own letter. Restless,

water poured over stone. Lichen. Burly skies. Punctuation of war zones.
What correlation of language here? How deep the evangelical?

Faith an evolutionary trait? What worth preserving, what ritual?
What breeding grounds? What remembered in the collective memory?

What words do we return to? Not yet, love. We are still arriving.
Protect me if I'm late. The calls are deafening.

Sound of rain on leaves. The deep and the shallows.
Endemic is what I meant to say. Refractory, raucous.

The night light's on. Somewhere there is something unfriendly lurking
and no one can protect you. Animal down, nothing to do.

In unsteady terms, what will be washed away, what makes every effort to stand, what awareness of system. Where does it get us except here in the constant engagement.

The steady, the not for sale, the been here before, the not dead yet, the debris, the roped off, the do not go there, the swim at your own risk, looms of destruction,

the advocacy of pain, the constable of it. Consternation, affable wounds, grass-backed will, necessary action of taking at some point,

the seizing of meaning, the inconstancy of it, the unetched superlatives, superstitious codes, the hazy zone. The mirror image. Sleeper cell.

Liebestraum. It's nasty out there. Tusk a doodle doo. Embryos. The painting of dust. Drift. The making up as we go along, slow jazz tune. Nothing set in stone.

Tell *that* to _____. The trappings. Bent knees. No vehicle. No motif. Thick skin on ground. The layman's prayer. Faces torn.

Levitation of souls, the bringing them around. Leaving them go. The invitation of it. The grim parts. Continued. Even if I knew the truth, I wouldn't

tell you not to listen, wouldn't twist the radio dial south. Listen, you should be livid. The evidence weighs in favor. Trust the turn. Light is erotic and shadow

and autumnal sun. I wish so in a lawless land. Grief has a scorecard, and it's picking us off. Leave it be, says the domino effect. But I don't want the question

answered. I want the question answered in questions. I want relief. What brilliant sleight of hand will bring you and me to the ground? Where the final edition? Finality

is banality. The end rhyme is right. Everyone knows the grit. Pitch. I carry out the bags behind a line of people counting their cash on Friday. Leavings happen.

Understatement, too. Smorgasbord, divinations. We are in a crux. A cradle. The moon shines brightly over most of us. Caravan. Numbers and notations.

Liaisons. Resonance, jewelings of drought. Flutter, genuine. Lockings down.

S

S

I have initiated the retreat.

It rights the boat, dumps the intrigues.

I do not trust myself with my own life, so hand me yours.

Slip knot.

I am voluminous,

a front.

The surplus affection we can certainly absorb.

Horror's lanugo,

the desiccation and the informant,

beads of morning sweat and annihilation.

The long tiger of wind.

I love you in language that has not yet been deciphered.

The one lost by the lost.

Love that looks at you as a plaintive animal.

Iodine applied,

your thoughts butterflies,

the billowing brilliance.

(Thank you for) This day's bread and butter.

The child and I are unanimous.

No letters of reference,

cord uncurling,

the meanings haven't fallen away, but been reinterpreted.

The feel of keys beneath fingers their easy resistance

the pressure of tongues.

T

T

I have found the trailway, the missing pieces still lost from me.

The seeping the spillage, air bristling. There will be no talk, no lightning,

no undertones of sleep, the body fluctuates and totters, slakes and wastes,

forcing the corners, hidden switches which remain flicked up but dark,

redeemable and sacrificial, sorted and unsorted,

the crowd call, the irrigated stumble, the unguided tour among ruins.

Souvenir stands blown over. The sovereign, the nomenclature,

pulse of power and attrition, the running,

this is feeling one's way in the light.

When living in the day to day is the tenebrous.

Yet I feel her burgeoning in water, evaporating until the dead

fall out of the sky like blessings.

I'd rather tend webbings, lace.

Not tend time but time's bearings.

I'm not quite sure nothing could be done.

The web continues in the longing. These pricks and prongs,

thought like breathing, happening all the time.

The absolution, the erasure

even in the folds.

I take the dead with me, in some way I inhale them,

hyacinth, I've been here forever, my unborn has been here forever,

waiting,

the shifting is forgiveness.

We scatter through mouths and minds,

transformed. What parts of us survive,

what happens to the rest except in the reverberation,

the subtle effects each breath makes and reciprocates—

U

U

The connection, even as we fall apart.

I bend, become grass.

The rising the lifting of hair.

Today is different, you can tell by the specificity.

The mismanagement forgotten. The irony zip-lipped.

The.

Sticky keys.

The gathering.

What I take back, scratched and slimmer.

This new precipice of intoxication.

In the placement and scatter of thistle, slumped houses,

establishing the lineage.

Love growing like tumbleweed.

The coming home country.

Fireflies, evening's phosphorescence.

Each day the watering. How life sets up for life.

Our kisses flash—

the whole contains the missing.

Slip into the crowd away from the crowd,

love made and re-made, wind path, stitch.

V

V

The better machine of your making.

The volume of commerce, blood,

which bodies matter more,

the bruising.

The vivisection I seek.

The seriousness of degree.

The wind cools me as I refrain from disaster.

My hands usually a breath from your veins,

their slick pathways and origins.

I was left to say goodbye.

To keep you irradiated while still there's breath.

And during the toxicity tests?

What will happen when you scream fratricide?

The bright shine of commonality. The usual spinal blocks.

The dismissing of griefs, angles.

Anecdotes surrendered on the table. You do the best you can.

The heart bends under weight of water.

The eviction notice as they then said.

Which people decide the fracture.

That's me lying there with the capacity to fall apart.

Infidelities of thought, calling like cicadas.

The provenance of doubt.

Visibility and demise.

Victory.

To render the lost words knowable.

The scent and touch of sore skin.

Vaulting out the window,

the veering. Into the perpetration,

the resurrection of belief.

My hands lax against your throat.

Skull nestled against collarbone.

You can write about love from any direction,

from the neck deep.

Our bodies' strong enclosure,

within and within and within

the velocity of days.

We the palimpsest, erasures layered and read,

like sedimentary rock, mutations.

Lovemaking tattooed deep in the body,

potent and light. Of conversation, damage, written up and over.

One kind ellipsis, where you find the answer—

The way the argument continues. The way you stretch open, *yes*.

W

W

The beauty of calling out.

Just as an aperture

a transfer of power,

operatic,

not a clasp but a coming around,

a bending backward into the remains.

In joining again the old traffic,

to skim and admire the old surfaces,

how does one renegotiate?

Wisteria, fence shawl,

orchid chandeliers,

climbing clear to the power lines.

The shortest distance between words is their utterance.

The grace of multiple peaks.

I am undone by my own intentions.

The entirety is left in its entirety,

someone always in bed with the other,

some village torched to the ground.

I slipped in shortly before daybreak

like a tongue that surprised you.

Is this what it means to go home?

The inscrutable you cannot enter, wind blowing,

house shuttered or worse, open and lit,

and still you cannot read its scripture,

breath-marks recognized and it resists you still.

The house burns and burns, and still the house stands.

X

X

The warmth annihilating. You were meant to be here.

I see your heart beating as the shadowy records suggest.

No exit wounds.

We go home to the home of the body.

The bottleneck of flowers.

A stem of birds hearkening.

A shift in pattern.

In the throat, hiss,

a downed shelter. What has no resolution

extends to its own points.

The draping leaves.

We go where we will go, into the undertaking.

Truth's black-eyed Susan.

To bless is to undo.

I am here in the delegation.

I am here to break open, like a wave.

Y

Y

Yarn over,

winter in the hand.

The nausea of leaving. Snow paddies, iced trees.

The heaviness not deceiving.

We begin to bargain.

Don't try and think it over. The altitude will do,

altering the way a body articulates thought.

The numbness will suffice.

Don't worry about the jagged peaks you're swept over.

They never find the body's feathers, its faded foliage.

Glory to whatever breaks free.

Z

Z

Have we reconciled now?

Do I shake your hand, kiss your cheeks, turn the other?

It takes place outside the language stalls.

This the place of contention, the ending, and the beginning.

Honesty, the interlock of scales,

shifting defenses, and entrances

I could not zero in on the hero's wake.

The holding of a child, watching the waves shift towards.

I'm where the sky ruminates, clouds gaze over us

expectantly, with great eyes.

To be watched at all angles, it dovetails, it crashes, it coincides.

What is it you see. What is it, exactly, I missed.

I hold you in my arms like a restitution.

As if the infiltration is over, what did not endure.

I hold you like the next bird calling.

The apparatus glowing. I have written all that I haven't saved up.

We know it. The primacy of seizure, undulance of sacrifice, of loving.

To figure out one's place among sound,

We start this way each time.

If you—

It's all right.

Finding our way in the stories.

To linger in the eventualities.

We dilate.

My friend caught a scorpion in his room this morning;

we do find our sharper points.

And the distance surges.

Adrenaline coaching the veins to superlatives.

The slip stitch of ice, the crunch of falling.

Lost whale calf calling for his mother.

The hollow, the long grief

of suckling a yacht,

death in open water.

The last time we saw so and so,

his name too painful to say.

The plain goodness of dreams,

the confessions made there.

We branch out, a tributary, spider veins.

The need for your blood wrapped round me.

It is you I love amidst all injuries.

I hold you in my light. The ramble of land.

This a matter of untiming,

a tending of days.

*

To feel like you never have to re-touch moments,

nor re-name plant or loss or event.

This resistance to severing.

The waves ultimately carrying us in.

No need to cultivate, make what was ours

ours again.

Where would you love me except in the here and now,

in the extension, the flowing back, the following.

We go to the far ends, a surface tension.

A touching of hands will suffice.

When I said the end I only meant an improvisation.

I used to think we were out there, and we are.

It is about the swell, the crease.

Cupboards empty,

what we fill with cake and hunger, replacing organs and bones,

we fill ourselves out with desire, we the rubbings,

the storm crop. The room upended with light.

We make love, bare boned as winter lightning.

The exteriority complete.

But the interior, sweet contagion,

I kiss your mouth rimmed with sugar.

Language I understand is in the tracings, rock beneath finger.

A train rattles the fence, the arbitration.

This flying flock of grain.

Scent of rain on pavement.

The body's wisdom.

I am drawn and drawn over

I invite you in.

How will we erase the erasures?

I won't be here when you arrive,

what I leave an approximation,

dry leaves, the sorting and sifting.

Which fight will pull you through like thread.

The lost translations no longer lost. Waves scudding by.

For in fragments come the dream.

For in the dream come the dreams,

almanac of love and weather.

A libretto joining the skeletal, what we abbreviate.

In the wilderness where we left off, anemone...

Note

pg. 50 "Because a circle opens in all directions" is from Arthur Sze's poem "Didyma."

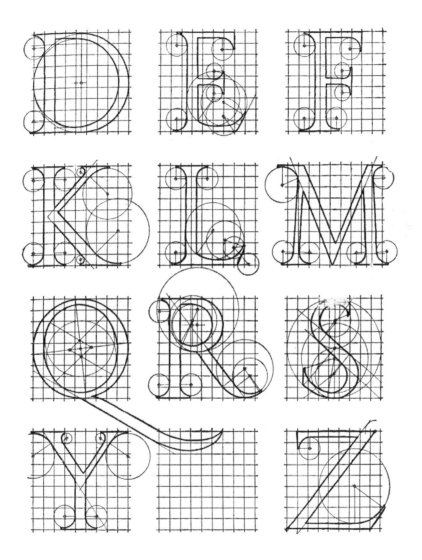

Stacie Leatherman is the author of two books of poetry and has an MFA from the Vermont College of Fine Arts. Her work has appeared in *Barrow Street, Caketrain, Crazyhorse, Diagram, elimae,* and *New American Writing,* among others. She blogs things literary and ecopoetic at stacieleatherman.com. She lives with her husband and son near Cleveland, Ohio.

Made in the USA
Lexington, KY
02 April 2011